California Real Estate Exempt Offerings

By: Douglas Slain, M.A., J.D.

Introduction

This handbook is addressed to anyone seeking up to $5,000,000 to fund a limited partnership where you do not want to specify which properties will be purchased and/or sold. This form of real estate partnership is known as a blind pool.

Just as in a blind pool real estate investment trust (REIT), investors in private placements do not know which properties the partnership will purchase. When you offer a blind pool limited partnership interest to a third-party, the evaluation of the partnership's prospects will be based on your track record as opposed to a specified pool limited partnership where prospects can be evaluated on basis of costs and projected revenues.

Interestingly, there is no evidence that the average performance of blind pools differs significantly from the performance of comparable specified pool partnerships.

For most real estate entrepreneurs the advantages of being able to raise money without having to first identify and have under contract a particular property are obvious.

Most real estate entrepreneurs I have known, when hearing the word "securities" associated with their deal, react as a 14th century Flemish townsman hearing of a new plague. But securities can be a good thing. Showing sophistication about the securities piece of your project can garner respect as well as expand the number of online prospective investors, to say nothing of giving you extraordinary advantages down the road if things go south.

Rather than speculate on what real estate projects may be best for blind pool private placements (location and timing), this handbook discusses subjects relevant to anyone looking for others to fund a real estate project when financial institutions are out of the question for whatever reason.

The first chapter explains why this subject may actually be of interest to you; to wit, unless your money partner(s) are also operational decision-makers, you are subject to California and possibly federal securities laws. You will learn why this is something your investors" lawyers can easily take advantage of if need be; see the Remedies for Investors discussion in Chapter Seven.

The next five chapters discuss the usual topics that need to be addressed in any effort to locate non-financial institutional money.

Chapter Seven highlights how easy it is for an investor to ask for the money back, at any time for any reason, if state (or federal) securities laws have been violated.

Chapter Eight constitutes an in-depth definition of the word securities as it applies to real estate projects and funds in California and other states.

Chapter Nine is specifically for California real estate projects.

Chapter Ten is a checklist of everything you could hope to put into a business plan. Chapter Eleven covers finders.

This is the first of two handbook covering popular uses of exempt offerings and private placements. The second handbook will be for EB-5 investment based immigration program candidates only.

Preface (Historical Note)

Most people do not know that individual states were regulating securities fraud before the federal government got involved. Years before the S.E.C. was a glint in the eyes of U.S. legislators, state regulators were shutting down securities violators.

The term "blue sky" suggests the type of fraudulent activity targeted by the states almost 100 years ago when Justice McKenna used the phrase in 1917 to characterize "speculative schemes which have no more basis than so many feet of „blue sky."

In *Hall vs. Geiger-Jones Co.*, 242 U.S. 539 (1917), the good judge wrote:

"The name that is given to the law indicates the evil at which it is aimed, that is, to use the language of a cited case, "speculative schemes which have no more basis than so many feet of 'blue sky'; or, as stated by counsel in another case, "to stop the sale of stock in fly-by-night concerns, visionary oil wells, distant gold mines and other like fraudulent exploitations'."

Even if the descriptions be regarded as rhetorical, the existence of evil is indicated, and a belief of its detriment; and we shall not pause to do more than state that the prevention of deception is within the competency of government and that the appreciation of the consequences of it is not open for our review."

While the SEC now is the chief enforcer of the nation's securities laws, each state has its own securities regime, known as its "Blue Sky Law," with its own enforcement apparatus in place.

Most states securities laws are modeled after the Uniform Securities Act of 1956; while some states may have identical statutory language or regulations, however, interpretations of the same words can differ from state to state. Before a security is sold there must be a registration in place to cover the transaction. Every offer or sale of a security must be registered or exempt from registration under blue sky laws of the state in which the security is offered.

Although many types of securities, and many transactions, are exempt from state securities registration under Regulation D (17 CFR § 230.501 et seq.), all states continue to require coordination or notice filings.

In any event, exemption never affects the ability of state regulators to investigate and to bring fraud charges. For some colorful examples of blue sky fraud, see enforcementreporter.com.

Table of Contents

Chapter One: Exempt Offerings

What is a private placement or exempt offering?

And why does it matter?

Shares of companies listed on public exchanges must have been approved by the S.E.C. and been qualified with state securities regulators. Those are public offerings.

If an individual or an existing company wants to be exempt from state qualification and Federal registration

when it raises money, it is a private offering. Such offerings include partnership interests and other familiar joint-ownership vehicles.

One example of a private offering is the Goldman Sachs ill-advised exempt (unregistered) offering of Facebook.com shares.

Another example was my neighbor asking a few fraternity brothers to invest $150,000 each in a commercial rental putative "flip."

Another example is a movie production and distribution start-up where one friend asks another for $50,000 to help launch it.

Small or big, sexy deals or prosaic, $250,000 real estate limited partnership or $250,000,000 next-big-thing pre—IPO Reg D offering (think LinkedIn and Facebook), they are all private offerings.

The easiest way to think of it is this: If you are asking someone for money for some venture in which you are to do the work and the other person and/or other persons are to receive some benefit from their investment, you have created a security.

Why does that matter?

Because securities have to be registered or be exempt from registration.

What if they are not? I know lots of deals where fear of "securities violations" had nothing to do with it. Some of these deals were very profitable for the investors and no one said a word about private offerings or "exempt" anything.

You are right; usually it does not matter! The vast majority of private deals are neither registered nor exempt from registration. In fact, so many private deals are not properly documented a state regulator once said, "There is a nation-wide crime wave going on and other than us guys no one knows about it."

Why bother to pay to do this right?

Because if the deal goes south, if anything at all goes wrong, whether or not it is the fault of the founder/owner/developer/promoter, you must return investors' money if they ask for it.

And if the money is not there, a judgment will be entered against the offeror no whatever how many LLCs or other entities were created to avoid just such exposure.

In other words, if you do not bother to get the securities compliance component right, any investor can ask for their money back, at a minimum.

This handbook provides useful information for individuals and companies who wish to raise money to do something entrepreneurial and not have to return the money due to a securities lapse. It also contains a chapter addressed to investors who want to take advantage of California"s Securities Act, serving as a cautionary tales for the entrepreneur as well.

Chapter Two: Business Plans

Business plans should be written as a form of deal evaluation.

Writing a good business plan is more than an exercise done to raise funds; it is an actual planning exercise, a thoughtful review of the viability of your venture.

View your business plan as a process to express your ideas as opposed to a chore you dread doing. Make your plan reflect your passion and commitment.

Communicate the viability of your idea but be modest in your promises.

Business plans written in this manner allow the integrity and sincerity of the writer to show through.

Investors will always reject exaggerated claims. After that, they will begin to doubt underlying business acumen and integrity.

A good business plan does not need to be long. Twenty to thirty pages often gets the job done. Do not start by writing the executive summary. Start with an outline of your ideas. Then write the plan. Then the executive summary should write itself.

Your executive summary should summarize the plan, not anticipate it.

Here is a template for organizing your thoughts.

I. COMPANY PURPOSE

II. THE PROBLEM

III. THE SOLUTION

IV. WHY NOW

V. MARKET SIZE

VI. COMPETITION

VII. PRODUCTS/SERVICES

VIII. BUSINESS MODEL

IX. MANAGEMENT

X. EXIT STRATEGY

XI. FINANCING

XII. EXECUTIVE SUMMARY

Chapter Three: Structure

What entity to use and how much of the pie for the investors and how much for you?

You understandably want to keep as much of the opportunity as you can for yourself. But if you miscalculate how much outsiders' money it will take, you run the risk of having to raise additional sums of money in the future rather than manage the business, or risk failing altogether.

You also need to decide which corporate entity to use. The tax advantages and flexibility provided by LLCs are well known; most real estate entities incorporate in Nevada or California.

Practice tip: It turns off investors when you get too clever in taking advantage of the flexibility of multiple LLCs.

Keep it simple.

Chapter Four: Private Placement Memorandum

Private placement memorandums (PPMs) are documents that disclose all relevant and material information that a reasonable investor would want to know when deciding whether or not to make an investment.

A PPM is different from a prospectus.

A prospectus is an offering document for registered securities. A private placement memorandum is an offering document used to sell securities exempt from registration under Regulation D.

The following information is background for understanding the law in this area.

Regulation D is a series of six Federal rules, Rules 501-506, establishing three transactional (that is, for the one transaction, not for the company itself) exemptions from the registration requirements of the Securities Act of 1933.

Rules 501-503 set forth definitions, terms and conditions that apply throughout the Regulation, while specific exemptions are set out in Rules 504-506.

Rule 504 applies to transactions in which up to $1 million of securities are sold in any consecutive twelve-month period. Rule 504 imposes no ceiling on the number of investors, permits the payment of commissions, and imposes no restrictions on the manner of offering or resale of securities. Further, Rule 504 does not prescribe specific disclosure requirements. Generally, the intent of Rule 504 is to shift the obligation of regulating very small offerings to state "Blue Sky" administrators, though the offerings continue to be subject to federal anti-fraud and civil liability provisions.

Rule 505 applies to transactions in which not more than $5 million of securities are being sold in any consecutive twelve-month period. Sales to thirty-five non-accredited investors and to an unlimited number of accredited investors are permitted. An issuer under Rule 505 may not use any form of general solicitation or advertising to sell its securities.

Rule 506 has no dollar limitation on the offering and it allows presentation available to an unlimited number of accredited investors. Rule 506, however, unlike 504 and 505, requires an issuer to make a subjective determination that each non-accredited purchaser meets a certain sophistication standard, either individually or in conjunction with a "Purchaser Representative."

Just as with Rule 505, Rule 506 prohibits any general solicitation or general advertising.

Almost all Regulation D transactions are offered pursuant to Rule 506.

Preparing a PPM pursuant to Rule 504, 505 or 506 commonly involves either a slightly modified version of your business plan surrounded by a significant amount of legalese, plus the subscription agreement, or a very condensed version of the business plan placed into the sea of legalese, including the subscription agreement, and then attaching the full business plan as an appendix.

NB: If you take the second approach, you need to make sure that there are no conflicts between your very condensed business plan and your full business plan.

Since you are still subject to state and federal anti-fraud statutes, the PPM must disclose all material information that a reasonable investor would wish to know before deciding whether or not to invest in your company or project. The reasonable investor standard is amorphous, as it must be.

Do this: Place yourself in the shoes of a potential investor and think about what you would want to know if you were considering investing. Everything you are thinking right now should probably be disclosed, especially if it is adverse to your venture.

Chapter Five: Preparing toRaise

You need an investor presentation. An investor presentation simply consists of your hand-outs (and power point presentation if you have one) for meetings with potential investors. Presentations are now commonly done by video conferencing.

A presentation can be structured as follows:

1. Describe your product or service and describe how it is better than competitive choices for the same service or product.

2. Describe key strengths that differentiate your product or service. Use graphics that shows how you provide everything that the competition does plus more; make a grid where the y-axis is your strength and the x-axis is the key benefit offered by your competitors(s), with your company and your competitor(s) each represented by a point on the grid-- with your company"s dot highest and to the right.

3. Describe how the cost of your product or service is less than the value of the benefit it creates, relative either to competitors' solutions or, if your product or service addresses an unmet need, to the current state of affairs for customer or clients.

4. Describe a desired future state for your customer that is more pleasurable (problem solved), more certain (problem avoided) or more fertile (new opportunity potential), plus the benefits (both performance and psychological) that the customer will receive from being in that future state.

5. Having described the value proposition of your product or service for a single customer, describe your initial target market, its scalability, and its dollars; total market and its dollars; and market category strategies.

    Include launch plans including branding and promotion theme, trade show opportunities, and public relations press release ideas.

6. Describe your sales strategy and distribution approach; include your direct sales force, channel strategy, sales cycle and/or unit pricing--and how that will change over time if it will.

7. Describe possible future versions of your product or service, and whether these new versions will allow you to provide a solution for additional target segments.

8. Present a 3-year projection of revenues, gross margins, earnings, and cash flow. Estimate the month and year you will achieve positive cash flow and positive earnings.

9. Explain the existing capital structure, who owns what, who will own what, and any unique terms. Explain why you need money now and how much money, if any, you may need in the future.

10. Communicate your valuation by expressing it as a multiple of revenues or earnings, using comparable transactions, or by some other method.

11. Recap by expressing, in new words that do not simply summarize what has already been said, why you have a credible growth story and why the investment risk versus opportunity equation is fair and reasonable.

Prepare a due diligence binder in which you collect in one place all of the pieces of paper that a seasoned investor might want to see to complete his due diligence, including copies of articles of incorporation, leases, employment agreements, option agreements, Keep in mind that it can take some time to complete this chore as the relevant documents may be located in numerous places. As with the presentation, you can work on the due diligence binder while completing other steps in the Reg D exemption process.

Finally, you need to file with the S.E.C. under Regulation D and file in each state in which you plan to contact investors.

Chapter Six: Raising Money

You are finally ready to raise some money. Who do you have in mind?

LinkedIn discussion group contacts?

Friends and family members?

Self-directed IRA seminars where you are one of several presenters?

Every time you identify a potential investor, send an appropriate email with your executive summary. Do not appear to be in a hurry. Record all contacts on spreadsheet. Follow up by telephone a few days later. You will get turned down most of the time, but some investors will ask for more information. At meetings, you will "present" as described in Preparing.

Typically, entrepreneurs spend weeks or even months researching, emailing, and phoning before they do much presenting but if you have your documentation organized go ahead and present as soon as you can.

There's no silver bullet, regardless of the quality of your deal. You can hire a finder in some form (see the last chapter of this handbook) who may be able to get you in front of people, but you will still need to present your business idea and yourself.

Chapter Seven: Charging Orders

Limited liability companies are the entity of choice for most entrepreneurs. They offer flexibility and some asset protection. Remember, however, that LLCs do not offer protection from securities fraud. There are two types of LLC creditors.

Inside creditors.

They can sue your LLC, but not you as an owner of the LLC. For example, someone falls and gets hurt on the LLC's property? They can only sue the LLC, not you.

Your residence and other personal assets are protected from inside creditors.

Outside creditors.

They can sue you, but cannot take your ownership interest in your LLC or take an asset owned by your LLC. For example, if you are sued after you caused a car accident, the victim cannot be awarded your investment in the LLC nor can they seize an asset owned by the LLC.

The LLC's assets are protected from outside creditors and if your LLC is sued, the best your adversary can hope for is a charging order.

A charging order only gives the creditor the right to any distributions of *profit*s from the LLC; it does not give away *the right to any cash distributions* if you choose not to make any—and the creditor(s) cannot force you to make them.

Further, since profit distributions are taxable, the outside creditor is an untenable possible: His debtor, you, can let the cash build up in the LLC while he must pay tax on it. [Yes, you read this right]. As a result, the last thing a creditor normally wants is a charging order.

The purpose of LLC charging orders is to protect the other members of the LLC not involved in that obtaining the debtor's membership interest, or the actual ownership of the LLC's assets, could adversely affect the other members of the LLC.

A foundation of LLC law is to not force other members of a LLC to have to deal with the creditor of each other.

This comfortable level of protection may soon be gone, however, in that a Florida Supreme Court has found that charging order protection is not applicable in the case of a *single member* LLC.

The court allowed an outside creditor to take ownership of several LLCs owned by the defendant, thereby gaining ownership of the assets owned by the LLCs.

This court ruled that the creditor should get gain ownership of the single member LLC (and thereby the assets of the LLC) rather than be forced to accept a charging order insofar as there were no other members to protect.

In other words, the court decided that no innocent partners would be adversely affected if the creditor were given the LLC interest. If you hold property in a single member LLC believing you have protected the property from outside creditors, think again.

While this is a Florida case, lawyers will immediately start to use the same logic to go after your LLC interest and assets in California and other states.

Even if you and your spouse are the only members of the LLC, creditors' attorneys will be arguing the same reasoning, especially in community property states such as California and Arizona where married couples are treated as a single entity.

The simplest protection is to add another member to your LLC or a third member if the only members are you and your spouse so that there is an unrelated party whose investment the court would need to protect.

However, never forget that no amount of asset protection planning will do a fig leaf of good against causes of action based on fraud.

Chapter Eight: Remedies for Investors

Investors who want their money back in California have state securities law and federal securities law on their side more so than they may realize.

Arbitrary arbitration does not have to be the outcome if you invested in an exempt offering that has gone south.

If you think you may have been mistreated as an investor in an exempt offering, first find someone who knows how to use the California state securities law ("the Act"), and then determine whether the Act applies to your transaction by reviewing Cal. Corp. Code Sec. 25008.

Note that a sale can be deemed to occur in California even when the purchaser is in another state or even when she or he communicates acceptance in the other state; see *Diamond Multimedia System., Inc. v. Superior Court,* 19 Cal 4 1036, 1050 (Cal S. Ct. 1999).

First Swing under the Act

Often you will find that an otherwise competent transactional lawyer failed to properly qualify an offering for an exemption. You are in luck.

The Act allows rescission of the entire transaction and all money back *even if your case is problematic* otherwise.

Ask for a certificate of non-registration from the California Department of Corporations. Under Cal. Corp. Code sections 25110 and 25102, the folks who sold you your partnership interest or other security must then prove that a valid exemption applied, as an affirmative defense.

Second Swing under the Act

Cal. Corp. Code section 25401 prohibits the offer, sale or purchase of a security through communications that include an untrue statement or omit a material fact.

Remedies under Cal. Corp. Code section 25501 include rescission or a suit for damages.

Importantly, note what is **not** required:
  proof of reliance
  proof of causation
  proof of defendant"s negligence

Rather, the affirmative defenses allowed under section 25501 are: a) proof that the defendant exercised reasonable care and did not know of the untruth or omission; b) proof that even if the defendant had exercised reasonable care, he would not have known of the untruth or omission; or c) proof that the plaintiff knew the facts concerning the untruth or omission. See *Bowden v. Robinson*, 67 Cal. App. 3d 705, 715 (Cal. Ct. App. 1977)

Damages Include Interest

In Boam v. Trident Financial Corporation, (1992) 6 Cal.App. 738, the Court held that recovery under the Act must be calculated as follows: "Consideration" + "10% Annual Interest" less "Income received" = "Recovery"

Damages Can Include More than Interest

Legal fees will be included if financial elder abuse is shown or as a component of exemplary or punitive damages.

If compensation to the adviser was based on appreciation of the assets, the client must have been a "qualified client" under Rule 205-3 (net worth in excess of $1,500,000).

Offering documents often confuse qualified investor qualifications with accredited investor qualifications— another legal give-me for the investor/plaintiff looking for a securities violation to get her or his money back.

More to consider is the fact that blue sky violations can lead to the law knocking. Most people are under the impression that securities enforcement actions are civil in nature. Although this is most often the case, a criminal prosecution can result if the facts are sufficiently egregious.

A person violates the law if he or she offers for sale or sells any security without registering the security, unless the security or transaction is exempted or the security is covered by federal statute. The Act exempts from registration certain securities, including securities issued or guaranteed by the United States and any state or political subdivision of a state, and other specifically listed types of securities.

Violations typically are punishable by merely fines, albeit stiff fines. However, other remedies may obtain, such as actions to obtain a temporary restraining order, temporary or permanent injunction, a declaratory judgment, the appointment of a receiver or conservator for the defendant of the defendant"s assets, rescission, restitution, or any other relief the court deems appropriate.

Chapter Nine: What is a Security?

California Corporations Code section 25401 reads:

"It is unlawful for any person to offer or sell a security in this state or buy or offer to buy a security in this state by means of any written or oral communication which includes an untrue statement of a material fact or omits to state a material fact necessary in order to make the statements made, in the light of the circumstances under which they were made, not misleading."

A security will be found when a person has invested value in a common enterprise with an expectation of profit to be derived from the substantial efforts of others.

This is sometimes referred to as the Howey test because of the United States Supreme Court"s decision in SEC v.

W.J. Howey (1946) 328 U.S. 293. The *Howey* analysis has been used by many California courts to determine the existence of a security.) *People v. Syde* (1951) 37 Cal.2d 765; *Tomei v. Fairline Feeding Corp.*)1977) 67 Cal.App.3d394; and *Moreland v. Department of Corporations* (1987) 196 Cal.App.3d 506.)

The second test is known as the "risk capital" approach, first used in California in *Silver Hills Country Club v.* Sobieski (1961) 55 Cal.2d 8111. That decision permitted the finding of a security when capital was sought from third parties which would be risked in a start-up of a business venture for profit. There was no requirement that an investor have an expectation of a monetary profit from the investment. The California Supreme Court emphasized the passive position as an essential element of the risk capital test.

The Howey and the risk capital tests are not mutually exclusive. Sometimes their elements are combined to determine whether an investment involves a security subject to registration in California.

(*Moreland v. Department of Corporations* (1987) 194 Cal.App.3d 506; see also *People v. Witzerman* (1972) 29 Cal.App.3d 169 and *People v. Schock* (1984(152 Cal.App.3d 379.) *People v. Corey* (1995) 35 Cal.App.4th 717 stands for the proposition, *inter alia*, that in a criminal prosecution for selling an unqualified, non- exempt security in violation of Corporation Code section 25110, the element of *scienter* need not be established.

Chapter Ten: Checklist

This business plan checklist is meant to be exhaustive with far more detail than required for most real estate funds. Let it serve to give you ideas. Just use what is practicable for your own situation.

I. *Management and Organization*

Describe who started the business and why. Explain the legal structure of the business.

Identify who will be the company's president. This is a required position in California, where a corporation must have a president, a chief financial officer, and a secretary, all of whom can be the same person.

Identify who will be the company's chief executive. This person will be viewed as the head of the company as well as the person who will run the company on a day-to-day basis.

Identify who will be responsible for the financial affairs of the company.

Identify who will be the secretary of the company. This person will be responsible for maintaining the company's books and records.

Describe the owners of the company and their relative ownership percentages.

Identify the directors of the company. Identify the board of advisers if any.

II. *Management Team*

1. Personal History of the Principals and Key Members of Management Team

List the business backgrounds of the principals and key members of the management team.

List the educational background, both formal and informal, of the principals and key management.

Resumes or curriculum vitae should be assembled and included for each of the principals and key management members.

Provide personal data for the principals and key management members, including age, current address, interests, education, special abilities, and reasons for entering into the business.

Depending on the amount of financing being requested, investors may require personal financial statements with supporting documentation for each of the principals.

2. Work Experience of the Principals and Key Members of Management Team

Highlight the past work experience of the principals and key management members, such as tracking successes, responsibilities, and capabilities. Make sure the information is complete and includes dates. Include resumes.

Identify any direct operational and managerial experienc in this particular type of business possessed by the principals and key management members.

Identify any indirect managerial experiences.

3. Duties and Responsibilities of the Principals and Key Members of Management Team

List the responsibilities of each of the company's officers and managers.

Explain who will do what and why (e.g., whether the company will have a director of sales and marketing or if those duties will be handled by another officer).

Consider whether some individuals have assumed more than they will be able to handle.

Provide an organizational chart with a chain of command and listing of duties.

Identify who is responsible for the final decisions and has ultimate responsibility.

Describe how many employees the company will need initially and at various points during its development.

State whether any positions will not be filled at this point in the company's development and explain the plans to address the situation.

Analyze and describe any known weaknesses in the company's anticipated management team.

List several possible solutions for the weaknesses.

4. Salaries and Benefits

Include a simple statement of what management will be paid by position.

List bonuses in realistic terms.

Describe any benefits available to the employees and owners that are to be offered through the business (e.g., medical, life insurance, disability).

5. Resources Available to the Business

List the company's supporting professionals, including its attorney, accountant, insurance broker, banker, and all other financial institutions through which business is conducted.

Identify the company's consultants who have been hired to deal with management, operations, finances, advertising, and other issues.

Identify the person responsible for the company's information systems.

Provide contact information to local business information centers such as chambers of commerce or the small business association.

III. *Product or Service*

Describe the company's product or service in as much detail as possible so that it can be understood by a lay person.

Explain why customers will buy this product or service Identify the benefits of the product or service and the need it fills.

Describe why the product or service is better than or distinguishable from directly competing products or services.

Describe the pricing structure for the product or service. Explain the product's life cycle and obsolescence. Describe the warranties for the product and/or service. Describe the company's guaranty policy, if any.

Identify any patents, trademarks, copyrights, trade secrets, licenses, or other proprietary information covering the product or service.

Analyze whether the company has the right to use the intellectual property necessary to produce the product or service and describe whether any royalties or other license fees will need to be paid to any third party to manufacture the product or service.

Describe how the product is manufactured or the service is delivered; indicate the facilities and equipment the company will need.

Identify the raw materials necessary to assemble the product or service, including any difficult to obtain.

Indicate whether there are any critical processes in the manufacture, assembly, or delivery of the product or service that have not yet been completed. If so, describe how much time and money will be required to bring the product to completion, and describe the risks associated with completion.

Identify whether the product or service will be enhanced in the future. If so, describe how much time and money this will require.

Indicate whether an example or prototype of the product can be included with the business plan without compromising confidentiality.

If not, analyze whether the product or service can be described in detail without compromising confidentiality.

Explain whether this product or service provides added value to another company's products or services.

Identify whether the company will develop future products based on this product and whether the product or service will need to be continually enhanced. If so, explain the resources that will be required to accomplish this and the time frames involved.

Describe what type of capital equipment the company will need.

Describe any parts or supplies that are difficult to obtain or that may require long lead times.

Explain the break-even point for the company based on its manufacturing and other fixed costs.

Indicate whether there are any government rules or regulations, such as environmental regulations, that may affect the company's manufacturing and assembly process. Identify any special permits that may have to be obtained.

IV.   *The Market*

Describe the market for the product or service and where the company's product or service fits within this market, as well as the "market segment" the company's product or service occupies.

Explain whether the company is competing on price or on other features.

Explain the due diligence that has been done to determine information about the market. For example, indicate whether reference works, government statistics and reports, books, and periodicals have been examined to gain an understanding of the market in which the product or service will be sold.

Analyze the company's strengths and weaknesses in targeting this market.

Describe the company's existing and prospective competitors. Indicate whether due diligence has been performed on each of those competitors to determine their strengths and weaknesses.

Explain how the company will deal with the strengths of each of its competitors.

Describe other products and services, even if not identical to the company's products or services that could fill the same need that the company's products or services will fill.

Describe how the company's products will be marketed to potential customers. Indicate whether the company has prepared a marketing budget and a timetable for accomplishing events necessary to meet its budgeted goals.

Describe the company's sales force, including the number of people necessary to accomplish the company's sales plan.

Indicate whether the company will sell through distributors, and if so, identify them.

Describe the total cost of sales for the company. Describe the compensation structure for internal sales employees (e.g., commissions, bonuses, and other benefits).

Describe the commission structure and discounts for outside sales people and distributors. Explain how the company will advertise its product or service.

Analyze whether the company will be able to secure "free advertising" via newspaper and magazine reviews and stories. Indicate whether the company will employ an advertising or public relations agency.

V. *The Competition*

Define the target market.

Identify closest competitors, including where they are located, what their revenues are, and how long they have been in business.

29

Identify the percentage of the market held by competitors.

Discuss how the company's operations differ from the competition, analyzing what the competition does well and where there is room for improvement.

Identify in what ways the business is superior to the competition and, alternatively, any areas where the competition surpasses the company. If the competition surpasses the company in any areas, to be credible the plan must identify those areas and explain how the company is planning on compensating.

Discuss how the competition is currently doing—specifically whether it is growing or scaling back.

Indicate whether financial statements for the prior 3 years, or for some lesser period of the company's existence, have been prepared by a certified public accountant (or prepared in accordance with generally accepted accounting principles). If not, explain why.

Describe the information from which the company will prepare its financial projections of sales, and all other income statement and balance sheet items.

Describe the assumptions underlying the financial projections.

If possible, provide a break-even analysis.

If possible, include *pro format* financial statements in addition to financial projections.

VI. *Presentation to Investors*

The plan should expressly state that it does not constitute a solicitation of an offer to buy or sell securities of any type and that such offer and sale can be accomplished only in compliance with applicable federal and state securities laws and regulations.

The plan should be concise. Investors may not bother to read it if it takes them too long to get through.

The pages should be in place. Errors in photocopying detract from the presentation.

The pages should be legible, especially the financial information, which should be in at least 10-point type.

The plan sections and documents within the sections should be indexed. Use of section tabs is recommended to allow the reader to easily flip between sections.

The numbers should add up. Verify that numbers used in projections add up to the correct results.

The pictures, if any, that are incorporated into the plan should be professional and attractive. Muddy or grainy shots detract from credibility.

All necessary information should be included.

All unnecessary information that does not directly advance the proposal should be omitted.

Avoid repetition.

Scientific or technical language that must be used is appropriate and definitions should be provided where necessary.

Additional references to the same item should be consistent.

Language used should be clear and concise. Avoid the use of jargon.

EXECUTIVE SUMMARY

Essential Contents

Provide a brief description of the company's history, if any.

State the company's objectives.

Provide a brief description of the company's products and services.

Identify the market in which the company will compete, including a persuasive statement as to why the business will succeed, discussing the company's competitive advantage.

Provide a brief description of the key management team. Describe the projected growth for the company and its market.

Provide a description of funding requirements.

Chapter Eleven: Real Estate Blind Pools

What real estate program and type of promotion can be done in California depends on which exemption you want to use, and that decision depends on how much money is being raised, the number of investors being sought, and whether the offering will be in more than one state.

I. The **California 25102(n)** exemption permits some advertising; $5 million maximum can be raised; it is limited to CA investors who are qualified investors but there is no limit on number of investors.

II. Qualified = $500,000 net worth, or at least $100,000 in gross income and $250,000 net worth (excluding residence), or a business worth more $5,000,000.

ADVANTAGE: TOMBSTONE DVERTISEMENTS CAN BE USED ON THE INTERNET AND IN PRINT.

Disadvantages: a) Company must be a corporation, not a LLC; b) **not available for blind pools;** and c) amount of investment of each individual cannot exceed 10% of his net worth.

The California 25102(f) exemption does not permit advertising but does permit prequalification of investors via Internet sites, blogs and seminars; unlimited amount of money can be raised and there are no financial requirements for up to 35 investors but they must be sophisticated or have substantial pre-existing relationship with company owner(s). As usual, there is no limit to the number of accredited investors.

DISADVANTAGE: REQUIRES (LIMITED) STATE REVIEW OF THE MERITS OF THE OFFERING

Federal Regulation D 506 exemption remains the gold standard even for small deals done intrastate, since: a) unlimited amounts of money can be raised; b) there are no financial requirements for up to

35 investors if they are sophisticated or have a substantial pre-existing relationship with company owner(s); and c) there is no limit to the number of accredited investors.

"Sophisticated" = reasonably assumed to have the capacity to protect their own interests in connection with the transaction.

"Substantial pre-existing relationship" = investor knows the company owner(s) well enough to be aware of any problems with the deal.

ADVANTAGE: NO STATE CAN REQUIRE A REVIEW OF THE MERITS OF A REG D OFFERING (AND STOP THE OFFERING)

What else can be done with a Reg D offering?

- Pre-qualification via Internet sites, blogs and seminars are permitted.

- Internet links to investor questionnaire and investor statements are generally permitted, but must be completed and returned before offering materials can be made available via password or other means.

- Seminars with only general information are permitted, with questionnaire following. (The SEC has said a comprehensive questionnaire is required, not just box-checking).

California real estate licensee?

California Department of Corporations Release 32-C provides guidance on how a licensed real estate broker can conform to Section 25201(a) of the Corporate Securities Law governing those who effect transactions in real estate securities in California.

Licensed real estate brokers are exempt from being licensed as securities broker-dealers if they sell interests in partnerships, joint ventures, or other entities (other than corporations) engaged in real estate development in California.

These "real estate entities" include entities that:

§ own land with no income producing capacity and with the objective of holding the land for development;

§ own and operate an apartment building or similar multiple-residential housing facility;

§ own and operate a building of offices or commercial space;

§ own a shopping center or industrial park offering units, sites, or spaces within the premises to lessees while not entailing or contemplating the conduct by the entity of any business within or in connection with the remises; and,

§ own motels, trailer home parks under certain circumstances; and agricultural land, under certain circumstances. If the entity engages in the conduct of a commercial, industrial, agricultural or other business or professional enterprise directly related, or incidental, to the ownership of real property, the entity will not be exempt. Some examples of this are the ownership and operation of a hotel, shopping center, or industrial park where the entity is involved in a business therein; other examples include owning and operating farmland with income derived from growing crops.

Chapter Twelve: Finders

Anyone faced with the challenge of funding a project from non-bank sources will ask this question sooner or later.

The law governing finders depends on whether you are engaging in a securities or non-securities transaction and, if it is a securities transaction, what type. You cannot know what rules obtain with respect to finders until you know the type of investor offering you are proposing.

If you are trying to raise money from a few active investors authorized to help make important management decisions, the use of finders is unregulated, as long as the finders do not negotiate the terms of the deal and compensation is disclosed. If you look for money any other way, you will be selling a security.

For a public or registered offering, or a public/private hybrid offering under the Model Accredited Investor Exemption, there is no pre-existing relationship requirement between the promoter and the investors. However, for a private placement offering management must have a pre-existing relationship with investors prior to the offering. In other words, you cannot rely on pre-existing relationships of finders in private placements.

The SEC''s general position is that receipt of transaction-based compensation signals broker-dealer activity, requiring licensing, unless the finder's activities are limited to merely introducing the buyer and seller.

Therefore, in deciding whether and how to use finders for your deal, the questions you need to ask are: Does the transaction involve the sale of a security or not? If a security, which exemption is being relied on at the federal level and which exemptions are being relied on at the state level.

About the author:

After getting a JD from Stanford Law School, a MA from the University of Chicago, a diploma from the University College London, and working as a reporter for The Wall Street Journal, Doug was a member of the California bar for 40 years, during which time he founded a series of law reporting services now owned by Thomson-Reuters. Doug specializes in debt and equity crowdfunding. He helps small business identify and solicit sources of private equity. Doug monitors a LinkedIn discussion group, State Securities Regulation, with 1500 members.

Connect with Douglas Slain:

LinkedIn: http://linkedin.com/in/douglasslain

Facebook: http://facebook.com/douglas.slain

Twitter: https://twitter.com/exemptofferings

Blog: http://www.privateplacementadvisors.com/apps/blog

Web site: http://privateplacementadvisors.com

www.ingramcontent.com/pod-product-compliance
Lightning Source LLC
Chambersburg PA
CBHW072046190526
45165CB00018B/1848